THE PORTABLE CRAFTER
CROCHET

THE PORTABLE CRAFTER
CROCHET

Carolyn Christmas

Sterling Publishing Co., Inc.
New York
A Sterling/Chapelle Book

Chapelle, Ltd.

Jo Packham • Sara Toliver • Cindy Stoeckl

Editor/Book design: Laura Best
Copy editor: Marilyn Goff
Photographer: Ryne Hazen
Photo stylist: Rebecca Ittner

If you have questions or comments, please contact:
Chapelle, Ltd., Inc.,
P.O. Box 9252, Ogden, UT 84409
(801) 621-2777 • (801) 621-2788 Fax
e-mail: chapelle@chapelleltd.com
Web site: chapelleltd.com

Library of Congress Cataloging-in-Publication Data
Christmas, Carolyn.
    The portable crafter. Crochet / Carolyn Christmas.
        p. cm.
    "A Sterling /Chapelle book."
    Includes index.
    ISBN 1-4027-1875-6
    1. Crocheting.   I. Title. II. Title: Crochet.
  TT820.C496 2005
  746.43'4--dc22

        2004025774

10 9 8 7 6 5 4 3 2 1

Published by Sterling Publishing Co., Inc.
387 Park Avenue South, New York, NY 10016
©2005 by Carolyn Christmas
Distributed in Canada by Sterling Publishing
c/o Canadian Manda Group, 165 Dufferin Street
Toronto, Ontario, Canada M6K 3H6
Distributed in Great Britain by Chrysalis Books Group PLC
The Chrysalis Building, Bramley Road, London W10 6SP, England
Distributed in Australia by Capricorn Link (Australia) Pty. Ltd.
P.O. Box 704, Windsor, NSW 2756, Australia
Printed in China
All Rights Reserved

Sterling ISBN 1-4027-1875-6

TABLE OF CONTENTS

INTRODUCTION

The crochet designs in this book were created with portability in mind. None of them require a large assortment of yarns, so you can pack a skein or two of yarn and this tiny book in your tote, and you'll be ready to stitch away whenever the opportunity presents itself. My personal favorite is crocheting while riding in the car or on a train. To me, there is something wonderfully relaxing and pampering about crocheting away while someone else takes care of the details of getting me from point A to point B. Time flies, and I'm constantly amazed at how much crocheting can be done during these moments.

While my three daughters were in school, I often took crochet along to pass the time spent waiting and watching games, practices, and other activities.

Crochet, at its most basic, is made up of very few variations of pulling one loop through another with a hook. Its simplicity and accessibility has made it an abiding pastime, as well as a method for creating necessities and decorative items, since the early 19th century.

With crochet, each stitch generally ends with only one loop left on the hook, so there is no worry of dropping stitches and unraveling work. If you make a mistake, you simply pull the thread end, "rip" back to the mistake, and crochet again.

Crochet is such a wonderful contemplative activity. Once you get going, most patterns have long stretches where you repeat the same thing over and again. Your fingers learn what to do, and your mind is free to wander far and wide, pondering the ups and downs of life. Studies have shown that brainwaves during crochet can be similar to meditation.

If you haven't crocheted in a while, the projects in this book are perfect for making crochet a part of your life again. You're certain to find more than a few projects here to make for yourself or to give as gifts. Most are not complicated and only the afghans require a significant investment of time—but even those work up amazingly quickly when approached one block at a time. Treat yourself and your loved ones to the snugly softness of crocheted hats, bags, scarves, and more—while treating yourself to the fun and relaxation of working with beautiful yarns.

CROCHET BASICS

YARN AND HOOKS

The yarns used in the projects in this book are merely suggestions for yarns that can be used to make the designs. Use your imagination and select different colors and fibers than the ones specified, keeping in mind that you should select the same weight of yarn as that specified in the pattern.

Yarns may be purchased in many places. Wonderful natural and synthetic fibers, in all colors and textures can now be found on the Internet, in craft and discount stores, and in yarn shops.

For most of the items in this book, a slight difference in size, which might be caused by a slightly larger or smaller yarn or hook, will make no difference.

However, for wearables, you will need to select yarn and hook size to achieve the specified gauge for an accurate fit.

Hook size specified in each pattern is meant to be used as a guide. Start with this size and work a gauge swatch where appropriate, and switch to a larger or smaller hook as needed to achieve proper gauge.

GAUGE

Gauge is measured by counting the number of stitches and rows per inch. It's best to make a gauge swatch several inches wide by several inches long. Allow your swatch to lie flat without stretching or pulling, and measure the stitches. If you have more stitches or rows per inch than the pattern's gauge specifies, switch to a larger crochet hook. If you have fewer stitches or rows per inch, try a smaller crochet hook.

PATTERN SYMBOLS

Most crochet patterns contain parentheses, asterisks, and brackets to indicate sections of pattern to be repeated.

Parentheses may enclose a set of instructions for stitches which are to be worked in one stitch or space; for example: (2 dc, ch 2, 2 dc) in corner space. Parentheses are most commonly used to indicate a series that is to be repeated a certain number of times; for example: (sc in next st, 2 sc in next st) 5 times.

Asterisks are most commonly used with parentheses, to set off a series of instructions which may contain a set of parentheses. For example: *Sc in next 5 sts, (2 sc, dc, 2 sc) in next st, dc in next st; repeat from * around. In this example, a single asterisk has been used. Asterisks may also be used in pairs; for example: *Sc in next 5 sts, (2 sc, dc, 2 sc) in next st, dc in next st *; repeat from * to * around. I often combine single asterisk repeats with a double asterisk, indicating a partial repeat at the end of a round or row. For

example, "*Sc in next 5 sts, (2 sc, dc, 2 dc) in next st **, dc in next st; repeat from * around ending last repeat at **."

Brackets may be used in instructions where parentheses and asterisks are already being used, and another symbol is needed to indicate another series of stitches or instructions. These are used in the same manner as parentheses and asterisks.

CROCHETING ABBREVIATIONS

Crochet patterns are written in the language of crocheting. These abbreviations are used for many of the repetitive words commonly found in crocheting instructions.

aft = after
bef = before
beg = begin(ning)
bet = between
bk lp = back loop
bp = back post
bpdc = back post double crochet
ch sp = chain space
ch(s) = chain(s)
chg = change
chging = changing
cl(s) = cluster(s)
cont = continue
dc = double crochet
dec = decrease
est = established
fp = front post
fpdc = front post double crochet
hdc = half double crochet
hk = hook
inc = increase
lp = loop
patt = pattern
pc = popcorn

pl = pull
rem = remaining
rep = repeat
rnd = round
sc = single crochet
sk = skip
sl = slip
sl st = slip stitch
sp(s) = space(s)
st(s) = stitch(es)
thr = through
tog = together
tr = treble crochet
yo = yarn over
* = repeat whatever follows *
** = end of repeat
( ) = repeat between ( )
[ ] = repeat between [ ]

Before beginning a project, read through the entire pattern. It will give you an idea of how the item is structured and you will be able to visualize the outcome easier.

There are detailed instructions at the beginning of a few projects when it calls for a stitch that may be unfamiliar. However, the majority of the stitches used are easily recognizable to a seasoned crocheter.

FINISHING

When all crochet pieces are finished, assembly is required for some designs. Sew seams by holding pieces flat with wrong or right sides together as pattern indicates, and hand-sew with a #16 or #18 blunt tapestry needle threaded, in most cases, with yarn used for crocheting. If you have crocheted with extremely textured yarn, sewing is better accomplished with a matching sport-weight yarn in a similar fiber.

Weave yarn ends in with the same tapestry needle. To weave ends, thread needle with yarn end and weave in and out under the wrong sides of a few inches of stitches. The larger the yarn you have used, the farther you should weave ends. For worsted weight and smaller, weave in at least 2". For bulky bouclé and textured yarn, weave under 3" to 4". Then weave in the opposite direction going through different strands. Cut end, allowing the end to recede into stitches.

If a project needs steaming or blocking, lay it flat on a table, bed, or ironing board, depending on the size of the project. Hold steaming iron near crochet, but not touching, and allow steam to penetrate. Using hands, smooth crochet, being careful not to burn yourself. Allow project to dry.

ORGANIZING MATERIALS

Because you will be moving your crocheting from place to place, you need a way to organize and carry all your belongings. Look for a bag that is large enough to hold your project, fibers, hooks, and other materials. A bag with various-sized pockets is helpful when organizing your materials. Canvas or fabric totes work well as do small backpacks.

BASIC CROCHET STITCHES
Slipknot (sl knot)

To beg crocheting, first make a sl knot. Make a loose knot at least 5" from end of yarn. Put end of hk thr lp (A); hk yarn and draw thr lp. Place lp on hk and pl yarn ends to close. (B)

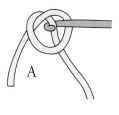

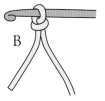

Holding yarn

To support the lp as you beg to st, hold your index finger up and pinch bottom of lp on hk bet thumb and middle finger.

Chain stitch (ch) on page 17

Place sl knot on hk. With hands in position (C) and with thumb and middle finger of left hand holding yarn end, wrap yarn up and over lp (from bk to front.) This movement is called "yarn over" (yo). Use hk to pl yarn thr lp already on hk (D). The combination of yo and pl yarn thr the lp makes 1 ch. Rep until desired length (E). Keep movements even and sts consistent. Hold hk near working area to avoid twisting. When counting, do not count the lp on the hk or the sl knot.

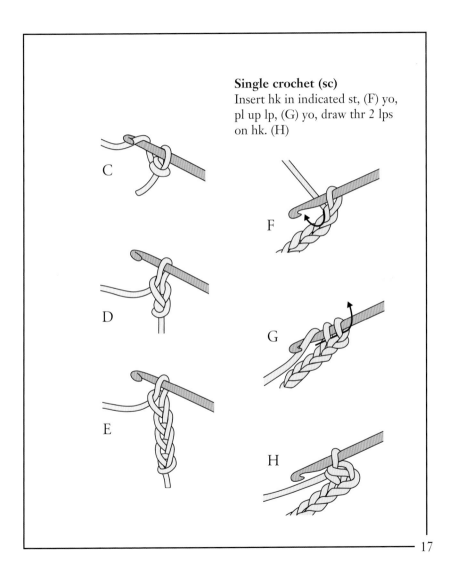

Single crochet (sc)
Insert hk in indicated st, (F) yo, pl up lp, (G) yo, draw thr 2 lps on hk. (H)

C

D

E

F

G

H

Single crochet next 2 stitches together (sc next 2 sts tog)

(Insert hk in next st, yo, pl up lp) 2 times, yo, draw thr 3 lps on hk. (I)

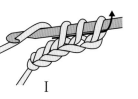

I

Slip stitch (sl st)

Insert hk in indicated st, yo; in one motion pl yarn thr st and thr lp on hk. (J)

J

Half double crochet (hdc)

yo, insert hk in indicated st, (K) yo, pl up lp, (L) yo, (M) draw thr 3 lps on hk.

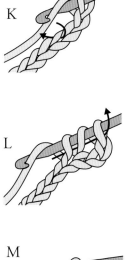

K

L

M

Double crochet (dc)

Yo, insert hk in indicated st, (N)
yo, pl up lp, (O) (yo, draw thr 2 lps
on hk) 2 times. (P, Q)

N

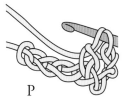

P

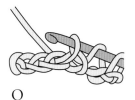

O

Q

Treble crochet (tr)

Yo 2 times, (R) insert hk in indicated st, (S) yo, pl up lp, (yo, draw thr 2 lps on hk) 3 times. (T, U, V)

R

S

T

U

V

Double crochet next 2 stitches together (dc next 2 sts tog)

(Yo, insert hk in next st, (W) pl up lp, yo, draw thr 2 lps on hk) (X) 2 times, (Y, Z) yo, draw thr 3 lps on hk. (AA)

Y

W

Z

X

AA

SPECIAL CROCHET STITCHES

Aside from the common crochet stitches already mentioned, there are a number of special crochet stitches used in projects throughout this book.

Back loop/front loop (bk lp/ front lp)

When working any st, insert the hk (BB) from the front into the back lp (1) or front lp (2) only of the indicated st.

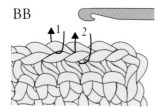

Front post double crochet (fpdc)

Yo, insert hk from front to back to front around next dc, (CC) yo, complete dc as usual.

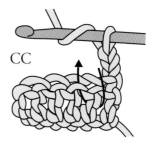

Back post double crochet (bpdc)

Yo, insert hk from back to front to back around next st, (DD) yo, complete dc as usual.

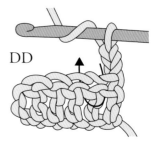

Skinny Scarf

NEEDED ITEMS
- Yarn: fuzzy textured bulky (1 ball)
- Crochet hook: K

GAUGES
5 dc = 1"
3 rows dc = 1¼"

SIZE
2" x 84" or length desired

INSTRUCTIONS

Row 1: Ch 4, dc in fourth ch from hk, turn. (3)

Row 2: Ch 3, dc in same st, dc in next st, 2 dc in last st, turn. (5)

Row 3: Ch 3, dc in each st across, turn. (5) Rep Row 3 until 1½ yards are left, or until desired length.

Next row: Ch 2, in next st (beg dec made), dc in next st, dc last 2 st tog, turn.

Last row: Ch 2, dc last 2 sts tog. Fasten off.

27

SUMMER TOP

NEEDED ITEMS
- Yarn: cotton worsted (3½ oz/186 yds/ball)
    A—Lt. Blue (3 balls)
    B—Lavender (30 yds)
    C—White (5 yds)
- Crochet hooks: G, H

GAUGES
6 rows patt st = 2"
7 patt sts = 2"

SIZE
Finished chest size: 32"
Instructions are in parentheses
    for sizes 36½" and 41"

SPECIAL NOTES
Est patt: Work (sc in next 2 dc, dc in next 2 sc) across, always working sc in dc and dc in sc.

INSTRUCTIONS
BACK
Row 1: With H hk and A, ch 57 (65, 73), sc in second ch from hk, sc in next ch, dc in next 2 ch, (sc in next 2 ch, dc in next 2 ch) across, turn. (56, 64, 72)
Row 2: Ch 1, sc in first 2 dc, dc in next 2 sc, (sc in next 2 dc, dc in next 2 sc) across, turn. Rep Row 2 until piece is 11½" (12½", 13" long.)

29

BEGIN ARMHOLE SHAPING

Row 1: Ch 1, sl st in first 5 (7, 9) sts, ch 1, sc in same st, work dc in each sc and sc in each dc across, leaving last 4 (6, 8) sts unworked, turn. (48, 52, 56)

Row 2: Ch 1, sk first st, sl st in next 4 sts, ch 1, sc in same st, work in est patt across, leaving last 4 sts unworked. (40, 44, 52)

Rows 3–: Work in est patt across 40 (44, 52) sts until piece measures 6½" (7", 8½") from beg of armhole shaping.

BEGIN NECK AND SHOULDER SHAPING

Row 1: Ch 1, sl st in first 3 sts, ch 1, sc in next 3 sts, work in patt for 7 (9, 9) more sts, turn. (10, 12, 12)

Row 2: Ch 1, sk first st, work in patt over next 9 (11, 11) sts, turn.

Row 3: Ch 1, sk first st, sl st in next 2 sts, ch 1, work in patt over next 6 (8, 8) sts, sl st in next st. Fasten off.

LEFT SHOULDER SHAPING

Row 1: Join with sc in 13th (15th, 15th) st from left edge, work in patt on next 6 (8, 8) sts, sc in next 3 sts, turn. (10, 12, 12)

Row 2: Ch 1, sc in first 3 sts, work in est patt over next 6 (8, 8) sts, leaving last st unworked, turn.

Row 3: Ch 1, work in patt on first 6 (8, 8) sts, sl st in next st. Fasten off.

FRONT

Work same as back thr Row 2 of armhole shaping. Rep Row 3 aft armhole shaping to work even in patt on 40 (44, 52) sts for 4 rows.

RIGHT FRONT NECK AND SHOULDER SHAPING

Row 1: Ch 1, work in patt on 13 (15, 15) sts, turn.

Row 2: Ch 1, sk first st, sl st in next st, sc in next st, work in patt across. (11, 13, 13)

Rows 3–9: Work even in patt.

Row 10: Ch 1, sk first st, work in patt over next 9 (11, 11) sts, sl st in next st, turn.

Row 11: Ch 1, sk sl st, sl st in next 2 sts, work in patt over next 6 (8, 8) sts, sl st in next st. Fasten off.

LEFT FRONT SHAPING

Row 1: Join with sc in 13th (15th, 15th) st from left edge, work in patt across, turn.

Row 2: Ch 1, work in patt across 11 (13, 13), sl st in next st, turn.

Rows 3–9: Work even in patt.

Row 10: Ch 1, work in patt over first 9 (11, 11) sts, sl st in next st, turn.

Row 11: Ch 1, sk sl st, work in patt on first 6 (8, 8) sts, sl st in next st. Fasten off.

ASSEMBLY

Sew side and shoulder seams; turn top right side out.

ARMHOLE EDGING

Rnd 1: With H hk, join A with sc in any st at bottom of armhole, sc in each st and in end of each row around armhole, join. Fasten off.

Rnd 2: With G hk, join B with sc in any st at bottom of armhole, ch 3, sl st in third ch from hk— picot made, sk next sc, (sc in next sc, picot, sk next sc) around, join. Fasten off.

NECK AND BOTTOM EDGING

Rep armhole edging.

FLOWER

Rnd 1: With G hk and C, ch 6, join with sl st in first ch to form ring, ch 1, 12 sc in ring, join.

Rnd 2: Ch 1, sc in first st, ch 10, (sc in next st, ch 10) around, join. Fasten off. Tack flower to the shoulder as shown below.

31

CHELSEA CAP & SCARF

NEEDED ITEMS

- Yarn: lightweight bulky (1 oz/60 yds/ball)
  - A—Eggplant (3 balls)
  - B—Camel (2 balls)
  - C—Red (2 balls)
  - D—Khaki (1 ball)
- Crochet hook: K

GAUGES

5 dc = 2"
4 rows dc = 3"

SIZE

Cap is 20" around; scarf is 92" or desired length

INSTRUCTIONS

CAP

Rnd 1: With A, ch 5, join with sl st to form ring, ch 3, 14 dc in ring, join. (15)
Rnd 2: Ch 3, dc in same st, 2 dc in each st around, join. (30)
Rnd 3: Ch 3, dc in same st, dc in next st, (2 dc in next st, dc in next st) around, join. (45)
Rnd 4: Ch 3, dc in same st, dc in next 8 sts, (2 dc in next st, dc in next 8 sts) around, join. (50) Fasten off.
Rnd 5: Join B with sc in any st, sc in each st around, join. Fasten off.
Rnd 6: Working in bk lps only, join C with sc in any st, sc in each st around, join. Fasten off.
Rnd 7: Rep Rnd 6 with D.
Rnd 8: Working thr both lps, join A with sl st in any st, ch 3, dc in each st around, join. Fasten off.

Rnd 9: Join C with sc in any st, sc in each st around, join. Do not fasten off.

Rnd 10: Ch 4 (counts as dc and ch 1), dc in same st, ch 3, sk next 4 sc, *(dc, ch 1, dc) in next st, ch 3, sk next 4 sc; rep from * around, join with sl st in third ch of ch 4.

Rnd 11: Sl st in ch-1 sp, ch 4, 4 tr in same sp, *sk next ch-3 sp, 5 tr in next ch-1 sp; rep from *around, join. Fasten off.

Rnd 12: Join B with sc in any st, sc in each st around, join. Fasten off.

Rnd 13: Join D with sl st in bk lp of any st. Working in bk lps only, sl st in each st around, join. Fasten off.

SCARF

Row 1: With B, ch 18, dc in fourth ch from hk and in each ch across, turn. (16)

Rows 2–48: Ch 3, dc in each st across, turn. Fasten off.

Row 49: Join A with sl st in first st, ch 3, dc in each st across, turn.

Rows 50–62: Ch 3, dc in each st across, turn. Fasten off. Turn

scarf and join D with sl st in first st on beg ch, ch 3, dc in each st across, turn.

Rows 2–15: Ch 3, dc in each st across, turn. Fasten off.

Row 17: Join A with sl st in first st, ch 3, dc in each st across, turn.

Rows 18–31: Ch 3, dc in each st across, turn. Fasten off.

FIRST END PANEL

Row 1: Join B with sc in first st, sc in each st across. Fasten off. Turn.

Row 2: Rep Row 1 with C.

Row 3: Rep Row 1 with D.

Row 4: Rep Row 1 with A.

Row 5: Rep Row 1 with C; do not fasten off, turn.

Row 6: Ch 4, dc in same st, *ch 3, sk next 4 sts, (dc, ch 1, dc) in same st; rep from * 2 times, turn.

Row 7: Ch 4, 2 tr in next ch-1 sp (half-shell made), (5 tr in next ch-1 sp—shell made) 2 times, 3 tr in last ch-1 sp, turn.

Rows 8–11: Rep Rows 6–7. Fasten off. Do not turn.

Row 12: Join A with sc in first st, ch 3, sc in sp bet half-shell and next shell, (ch 3, sk next 2 tr, sc in next tr, ch 3, sc in sp bet shells) 2 times, ch 3, sk next 2 tr, sc in last tr. Fasten off.

Work same as first end panel, except work this color order for Rows 1–4: D, B, C, A.

BABY CUPCAKE HAT

NEEDED ITEMS
- Yarn: baby-weight or sport-weight
  - A—Blue
  - B—Lime
  - C—Coordinating speckled
- Crochet hook: F

GAUGES
5 dc = 1"
3 rows dc = 1¼"

SIZE
Fits head size 12"–15" around

SPECIAL NOTES
To chg colors, pl new color thr last 2 lps of indicated st.

INSTRUCTIONS

RIBBING
Row 1: Ch 11 with A, sc in second ch from hk, sc in each ch across, turn. (10)
Row 2: Working in bk lps only, ch 1, sc in each st across, chging to B in last st, turn. Do not cut A.
Row 3: Working in bk lps only, ch 1, sc in each st across, turn.
Row 4: Working in bk lps only, ch 1, sc in each st across, chging to A in last st, turn. Do not cut B.
Rows 5–64: Rep Rows 3 and 4 for patt, chging colors on every other row, until there are 16 stripes of each color. Turn, working in bk lps only of last row, sl st last row to beg ch, forming ring. Fasten off.

HAT
Rnd 1: Hold ribbing with edge at top where yarn colors were carried along edge; work this rnd over carried strands. Join C with sl st in end of any row, ch 3, work dc in end of each row around, join with sl st in top of ch 3. (64)

Rnd 2: Ch 3, dc in each st around, join, chging to B. Do not cut C; drop to back of work.

Rnd 3: With B, ch 1, sc in first st, sc in each st around, join. Fasten off.

Rnd 4: Draw C thr first st, ch 3, dc in each st around to last 2 sts, dc last 2 sts tog, join.

Rnd 5: Ch 3, dc in next 7 sts, chging to A in last 2 lps of last st; with A, working over C strand, 5 dc in next st chging to C in last dc, remove hk from lp, insert hk in top of first of 5 dc just made, draw dropped lp thr (A pc made), *with C, working over A strand, dc in next 8 sts chging to A in last 2 lps of last st, working over C strand, make A pc, rep from * around, join. Fasten off A.

Rnd 6: With C, ch 3, dc in each st around, join. Fasten off.

Rnd 7: Join B with sc in any st, sc in each st around, join. Fasten off.

HAT TOP

Rnd 1: With A, ch 5, join with sl st to form ring, ch 3, 14 dc in ring, join. (15)

Rnd 2: Ch 3, dc in same st, 2 dc in each st around, join. (30)

Rnd 3: Ch 3, dc in same st, dc in next st, (2 dc in next st, dc in next st) around, join. (45)

Rnd 4: Ch 3, dc in next st, 2 dc in next st, (dc in next 2 sts, 2 dc in next st) around, join. (60)

Rnd 5: Ch 3, dc in same st, (dc in next 20 sts, 2 dc in next st) 2 times, dc in each rem st around, join. (63)

JOINING TOP TO HAT

Hold wrong side of Rnd 5 of hat top to wrong side of Rnd 7 of hat. Work thr both layers, with A, sc in each st around, join. Fasten off.

TOP PUFF

Rnd 1: With C, leaving tail, ch 5, join with sl st in first ch to form ring, ch 1, 8 sc in ring, do not join, work in rnds. (16)

Rnd 2: 2 sc in each st around, join. (16)

Rnds 3–4: Sc in each st around, join.

Rnd 5: (Sc next 2 sts tog) around, stuffing lightly with yarn tail bef closing. Sl st in next st. Fasten off.

FINISHING

Sew top puff to center of hat top.

Citrus Baby Afghan

NEEDED ITEMS
- Yarn: baby-weight or sport-weight (12 oz)
- Crochet hook: G

GAUGE
Block = 3" sq

SIZE
Afghan = 29½" sq

INSTRUCTIONS

FIRST BLOCK

Rnd 1: Ch 6, join with sl st in first ch to form ring, ch 3, 15 dc in ring, join with sl st in top of ch 3. (16)

Rnd 2: Ch 1, sc in same st, ch 3, sk next st, (sc in next st, ch 3, sk next st) around, join.

Rnd 3: Sl st in next ch-3 sp, ch 3, (dc, ch 2, 2 dc) in same sp, (2 dc, ch 2, 2 dc) in each ch-3 sp around, join.

Rnd 4: Sl st in next dc, sl st in next ch-2 sp, ch 3, (3 dc, ch 3, 4 dc) in same ch-sp, ch 3, sc in next ch-2 sp, ch 3, *(4 dc, ch 3, 4 dc) in next ch-2 sp, ch 3, sc in next ch-2 sp, ch 3; rep from * around, join. Fasten off.

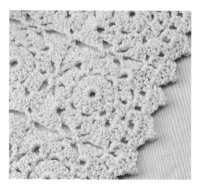

SECOND BLOCK

Rnds 1–3: Work same as first block.

Rnd 4: Sl st in next dc, sl st in next ch-2 sp, ch 3, (3 dc, ch 3, 4 dc) in same ch-sp, ch 3, sc in next ch-2 sp, ch 3; to work joining side, [4 dc in next ch-2 sp, ch 1, sl st in ch-3 sp on corner of first block, ch 1, 4 dc in same ch-sp on second block], ch 1, sl st in next ch-3 sp on first block, ch 1, sc in next ch-2 sp on second block, ch 1, sl st in next ch-3 sp on first block, ch 1; rep bet [ ]; ch 3, sc in next ch-2 sp, ch 3, (4 dc, ch 3, 4 dc) in next ch-2 sp, ch 3, sc in next ch-2 sp, ch 3, join. Fasten off.

REMAINING BLOCKS

Work same as second block, work-ing joining sides as needed to join 81 blocks in a nine-by-nine block grid.

BORDER

Rnd 1: Join with sl st in a corner ch-3 sp, ch 3, (2 dc, ch 3, 2 dc) in same corner, *ch 1, sk next dc, dc in next 2 dc, (ch 1, 2 dc in next ch-3 sp) 2 times, ch 1, sk next dc, dc in next 2 dc, ch 1, 2 dc in next corner ch-3 sp on this block, ch 1, 2 dc in first corner ch-3 sp on next block; rep from * around with (2 dc, ch 3, 2 dc) in each corner of afghan, join.

Rnd 2: Sl st in next dc, sl st in corner ch-3 sp, ch 4, (dc, ch 1, dc, ch 3, sl st in third ch from hk—picot made—dc, ch 1, dc, ch 1, dc) in same corner sp, *sc in next ch-1 sp, [(dc, ch 1, dc, picot, dc, ch 1, dc) in next ch-1 sp, sc in next ch-1 sp]; rep bet [ ] across to corner sp, (dc, ch 1, dc, ch 1, dc, picot, dc, ch 1, dc, ch 1, dc) in corner sp, rep from * around, join. Fasten off.

PANACHE PURSE

NEEDED ITEMS
- Yarn:
    A—super bulky, Multicolor (171 yds)
    B—eyelash, Red (60 yds)
    C—cotton crochet thread, size 10, Red (30 yds)
- Crochet hooks: G, H, K
- ¼" Button (1)
- Magnetic snap (optional)

GAUGES
2 dc = 1"
1 row dc = 1"

SIZE
15" wide at highest point x 11"
high plus handle

INSTRUCTIONS
PURSE BACK AND FLAP
Row 1: Beg at point of flap, with
K hk and main color, ch 4, 2 dc in
fourth ch from hk, turn. (3)

Row 2: Ch 3, dc in same st, dc
in next st, 2 dc in last st, turn. (5)
Row 3: Ch 3, dc in same st, dc
in each st across with 2 dc in last
st. (7)
Rows 4–17: Rep Row 3. (35 dc
on Row 17)
Rows 18–21: Ch 3, dc in each
dc across, turn. (35)
Row 22: Sl st in first 7 sts, ch 3,
dc in next 22 sts, turn, leaving last
6 sts unworked. (23)
Row 23: Ch 3, dc in each st
across. Fasten off.

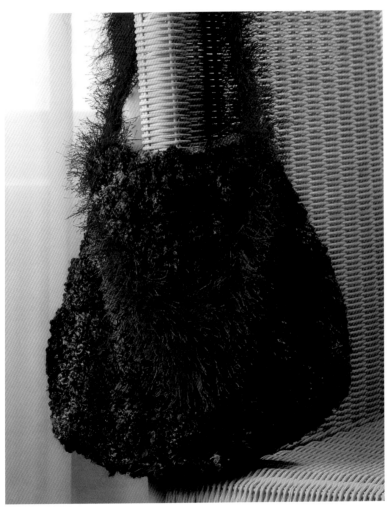

PURSE FRONT

Row 1: Ch 25, dc in fourth ch from hk, dc in each ch across, turn. (23)

Row 2: Ch 3, dc in same st, dc in each st across with 2 dc in last st. (25)

Rows 3–7: Rep Row 2. (35 dc on Row 7)

Rows 8–13: Rep Rows 18–23 of back and flap.

ASSEMBLY

Using C for sewing, holding front and back tog and aligning bottom edges, sew ends of Rows 1–11 on front to ends of Rows 11–21 on back for side seams. Sew center 23 sts tog for bottom center seam. Align side seam with bottom seam on each edge and align ends of last 2 rows to 6 unworked sts on each side to form boxed bottom shaping. Sew seams perpendicular to center bottom and side seams. Turn purse right side out.

TRIM

Rnd 1: Holding purse with inside of front-top edge facing you, with H hk and working with one strand C and one strand B held tog, join with sl st in any st. Working from wrong side, working around front edge and all around flap edge, ch 2, hdc in same st, 2 hdc in each st and in end of each row around with 5 hdc at flap point, join.

Rnd 2: Ch 2, hdc in next st, hdc in each st around, join. Fasten off.

BUTTON COVER

Rnd 1: With G hk and working with one strand C and one strand B held tog, ch 5, join with sl st to form ring, ch 1, 7 sc in ring, do not join, work in rnds.

Rnd 2: 2 sc in each st around. (14)

Rnd 3: (2 sc in next sc, sc in next sc) around. (21)

Rnd 4: Sc in each sc around, sl st in next sc. Fasten off leaving tail. Shake piece vigorously to fluff eyelash. Wrong side of crochet piece will be right side of finished button; weave in all ends except outside tail of crochet cotton thread. Thread needle with tail. Holding button against wrong side, weave needle in and out of

Row 2: Ch 2, fpdc around each dc across. Fasten off.

Sew handle ends to top sides of purse, sewing on inside.

Following package instructions, affix magnetic snap to flap point and to corresponding position on purse body.

Sew covered button to back of magnetic snap on outside of purse flap. Take care not to pl on sts when opening purse with magnetic snap.

last rnd of sts, pl tight to cinch button cover over button. Take a few small sts to secure.

HANDLE

Row 1: With H hk and working with one strand C and one strand B held tog, ch 100, dc in fourth ch from hk, dc in each ch across, turn.

45

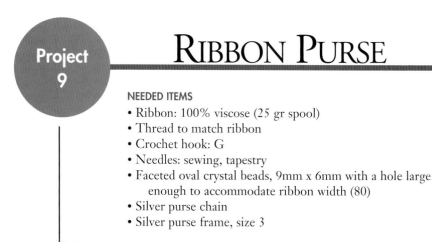

RIBBON PURSE

NEEDED ITEMS
- Ribbon: 100% viscose (25 gr spool)
- Thread to match ribbon
- Crochet hook: G
- Needles: sewing, tapestry
- Faceted oval crystal beads, 9mm x 6mm with a hole large
  enough to accommodate ribbon width (80)
- Silver purse chain
- Silver purse frame, size 3

Designed by Whitney Christmas

SIZE
Finished purse: 3" x 4"

INSTRUCTIONS
String all beads onto ribbon.
Row 1: Ch 35, sc in second ch from hk, sc in each ch across, turn. (34)
Row 2: Ch 1, sc in each sc across, turn.

Rows 3–4: Ch 1, sc in first st, dc in next st, (sc in next st, dc in next st) across, turn.
Row 5: Ch 1, sc in each st across.
Row 6: Ch 1, sc in first st, slide bead up to hk, insert hk in next st, yo, pl up lp, yo, pl thr 2 lps on hk—beaded sc made, (sc in next st, beaded sc in next st) across, turn.
Row 7: Ch 1, sc in each st across, turn.

Rows 8–13: Rep Rows 3–7.
Rows 14–15: Rep Rows 6–7.
Rows 16–21: Rep Rows 3–7.
Rows 22–23: Rep Rows 3–4.
Rows 24–25: Ch 1, sc in each st across, turn. Fasten off.

FINISHING

Weave in all ends. Fold crochet piece lengthwise and sew side seams. With bag right side out, line up one seam with hinge; baste to hinge if desired. *Sew from hinge to first corner, easing to fit. The first row of beads should be placed right aft the first corner. Ease to fit along top edge of frame with all bead rows placed on the long flat edge of frame. Sew piece to next hinge. Rep from * for rem side.

Attach 9½" of chain for handle, using the jump rings that come with handle.

CHERRIES PILLOW

NEEDED ITEMS
• Yarn:
    A—worsted acrylic or wool blend, White or White
     Frosted (5 oz)
    B—worsted chenille, Red (1 oz)
    C—worsted chenille, Sage green (1 oz)
• Crochet hooks: G, H
• Pillow form, 12"

GAUGES
7 dc = 2"
3 rows dc = 2"

SIZE
12" sq plus ruffle

INSTRUCTIONS
PILLOW FRONT
Row 1: With H hk and A, ch 41, sc in second ch from hk, dc in next ch, (sc in next ch, dc in next ch) across, turn. (40)
Row 2: Ch 1, sc in first dc, dc in next dc, (sc in next dc, dc in next sc) across, turn.
Rows 3–: Rep Row 3 until piece is square. Fasten off.

PILLOW BACK
Pillow back may be made same as front, or as follows:
Row 1: With H hk and A, ch 42, dc in fourth ch from hk, dc in each ch across, turn. (40 dc)
Row 2: Ch 3, dc in next dc, dc in each dc across, turn. (40)
Rows 3–: Rep Row 3 until piece is square. Fasten off.

ASSEMBLY
Rnd 1: Holding pillow front and back wrong sides tog and working thr both layers, join A with sc in any st, sc in each sc, sc in end of each sc row, and 2 sc in end of each dc row around with 3 sc in

49

each corner, inserting pillow form bef closing, join. Fasten off.

RUFFLE
Rnd 1: With G hk, join B with sc in any st along edge, ch 3, (sc in next st, ch 3) around, join. Fasten off.
Rnd 2: Join C with sc in any ch-3 lp, ch 3, (sc in next ch-3 lp, ch 3) around, join. Fasten off.

CHERRIES (MAKE 5)
Rnd 1: With G hk and B, ch 5, join with sl st in first sc to form ring, ch 1, 8 sc in ring, do not join, work in rnds. (8)
Rnd 2: 2 sc in each sc around. (16)
Rnds 3–4: Sc in each sc around. (16)
Rnd 5: (Sc next 2 sts tog) around, stuffing lightly with matching scrap yarn bef closing. Sl st in next st. Fasten off.

DOUBLE STEM (MAKE 2)
With G hk and C, ch 20. Fasten off, leaving tail for sewing.

SINGLE STEM (MAKE 1)
With G hk and C, ch 10. Fasten off, leaving tail for sewing.

FINISHING
Flattening cherries slightly, sew to background. Folding double stems slightly off center in half, sew in place as shown in the photograph below. Sew single stem in place.

MOEBIUS WRAP

NEEDED ITEMS
- Yarn: mohair-blend sport (7½ oz)
- Crochet hook: H
- Needle: darning

GAUGE

5 rows dc = 3"; dc = 1"

SIZE

15" long; fits around any size shoulders

INSTRUCTIONS

Rnd 1: Loosely ch 145 or number of chains needed to fit around shoulders, dc in fourth ch from hk, dc in each ch across. At end of row, lay strip on flat surface and bring ends tog; working into opposite side of starting ch, sl st in base of ch-3 at beg of rnd, sc in next ch, hdc in next ch, dc in each rem ch around.

Rnd 2: Dc in top of ch 3 at beg of Rnd 1 (this leaves a small opening which will be sewn closed later), dc in each st around; do not join, work in rnds. This never-ending strip shows the wrong side of rows on one side and right side of rows on the other. Cont with dc in each st around until wrap is 11"–12" long or 4"–5" less than desired length. At end of last rnd, hdc in next st, sc in next st, sl st in next st. Do not fasten off.

BORDER

Rnd 1: Sk next 2 sts, ch 3, 2 dc in same st, sk next 2 sts, (3 dc in next st—shell made, sk next 2 sts) around, join.

Rnds 2–3: Sl st in next dc, ch 3, 2 dc in same st, (3 dc in center dc of next shell) around, join. Fasten off.

FINISHING

Using yarn tail, sew opening on Rnd 2 closed. Steam wrap to alleviate curling edges.

59

SUMMER HAT

NEEDED ITEMS
- Yarn: cotton baby (2½ oz)
- Crochet hook: F

SIZE
Fits ages 4–6

INSTRUCTIONS
Rnd 1: Ch 5, join with sl st in first ch to form ring, ch 3, 11 dc in ring, join in top of ch-3. (12)
Rnd 2: Ch 3, dc in same st, 2 dc in each st around, join. (24)
Rnd 3: Ch 3, dc in same st, dc in next 2 sts, (2 dc in next st, dc in next 2 sts) around, join. (36)
Rnd 4: Ch 3, dc in same st, dc in next 3 sts, (2 dc in next st, dc in next 3 sts) around, join. (48)
Rnd 5: Ch 3, dc in same st, dc in next 4 sts, (2 dc in next st, dc in next 4 sts) around, join. (60)
Rnd 6: Ch 3, dc in same st, dc in next 5 sts, (2 dc in next st, dc in next 4 sts) around, join. (72)
Rnds 7–10: Ch 3, dc in next st, dc in each st around, join. (72)
Rnd 11: Ch 1, sc in same st, sk next st, 3 dc in next st, sk next st, (sc in next st, sk next st, 3 dc in next st, sk next st) around, join.
Rnds 12–13: Sl st in next 2 dc, ch 1, sc in same st, (3 dc in next sc, sc in center dc of next 3-dc group) around, join with sl st in first sc.
Rnd 14: Sl st in next 2 dc, ch 1, sc in same st, (5 dc in next sc, sc in center dc of next 3-dc group) around, join.
Rnd 15: Ch 1, sc in same st, *dc in next dc, (ch 1, dc in next dc) 4 times**, sc in next sc; rep from * around, ending last rep at **, join.
Rnd 16: Ch 1, sc in same st, *(ch 3, sc in next ch-1 sp) 4 times, ch 3**, sc in next sc; rep from ** around, ending last rep at **, join. Fasten off.

FINISHING (OPT)
Embellish with crocheted flowers, buttons, or other items.

61

FUR CUSHION

NEEDED ITEMS
- Yarn:
  A—bulky (185 yds)
  B—eyelash, coordinating color (120 yds)
- Crochet hook: L
- Needle: tapestry
- Foam cushion form, 12" x 12" x 2"

SIZE
12" sq

INSTRUCTIONS

Rnd 1: Holding 1 strand A and 2 strands B tog, ch 61, sc in second ch from hk and in each ch across; being careful not to twist row, sc in first sc on row, forming ring. Do not join rnds; work in rnds.

Rnds 2– : Sc in each sc around, continuing until piece is 12" tall. Turn piece inside out (back of sc is right side). Shake vigorously to release eyelashes. Do not fasten off. Flatten end; working thr both layers, sc in 30 sts across, closing end seam. Fasten off.

FINISHING

Insert foam cushion. Flatten rem end seam, working thr both layers, join with sc at side, sc in 30 sts across. Fasten off. With yarn tail, sew opening at end of Rnd 1 closed.

63

CHERRIES PURSE

NEEDED ITEMS
- Cotton crochet threads:
    A—size 3, Black (450 yds)
    B—size 10, Red (5 yds)
    C—size 10, Green (5 yds)
- ½" dia. cotton cord (30")
- Steel crochet hooks: 0, 7
- Needle: sewing
- Thread to match

Designed by Elizabeth Ann White

SIZE
10" wide x 7½" high plus handles

INSTRUCTIONS

PURSE

Rnd 1: With A and larger hk, (ch 3, dc in third ch from hk) 15 times, ch 6, sl st in sixth ch from hk; working in ch sps and over sides of dcs, sl st in second sp from end, 3 sc in each sp across to opposite end, 6 sc in last sp; working on opposite side, 3 sc in each sp across, 6 sc in last sp, join with sl st in first sc. (96)

Rnd 2: Ch 1, sc in first 42 sts, 2 sc in each of next 6 sts, sc in next 42 sts, 2 sc in each of last 6 sts, join. (108)

Rnds 3–15: Ch 1, sc in each st around, join.

Rnd 16: Ch 1, sc in first st, sk next 2 sts, 5 dc in next st, sk next 2 sts, (sc in next st, sk next 2 sts, 5 dc in next st, sk next 2 sts) around, join.

Rnds 17–30: Sl st to center dc of next 5-dc group, ch 1, sc in same st, 5 dc in next st, (sc in center dc of next 5-dc group, 5 dc in next sc) around, join. At end of last rnd, fasten off.

HANDLE (MAKE 2)

Rnd 1: Working around 15"
piece of cord, with larger hk
and A, leaving tail for sewing,
ch 8, join with sl st in first ch to
form ring, sc in each ch around;
do not join, work in rnds.

Rnd 2: Sc in each st around.

Rnds 3–: Rep Rnd 2 until cord is
covered. (If it is more comfortable
for you, you can complete the
crochet, then pl cord thr using
safety pin.) At end of last rnd, sl st
in next st. Fasten off.

ASSEMBLY

Sew ends of handles closed, using
thread tails. Sew handles to inside
top of purse.

CHERRIES (MAKE 5)

Cut 5 pieces of B, each 1 yard
long.

Rnd 1: With B and smaller hk,
ch 2, sc in second ch from hk,
do not join.

Rnd 2: 2 sc in each st around.

Rnds 3–5: Sc in each st around.

Rnd 6: (Sc next 2 sts tog) 6 times.
Fasten off, leaving tail for sewing.
Stuff with thread cut from piece
when fastening off. With thread
tail, weave thr sts of last rnd; pl
tight to close opening, and take a
couple of small sts to secure and
hide thread end inside cherry.

LEAVES AND STEMS
First leaf

Row 1: With C and smaller
hk, ch 4, 4 dc in fourth ch from
hk, turn.

Rows 2–3: Ch 3, dc in each st
across, turn.

Row 4: Ch 2, (yo, pl up lp in next
dc, yo, pl thr 2 lps on hk) 3 times,
yo, pl thr all lps on hk—3 dc dec
made, ch 3, sl st in last st; working
across ends of Rows 1–3, (ch 3, sl

st in base of last st on next row)
3 times; do not fasten off.

Second leaf
Row 1: Ch 4, 4 dc in fourth ch
from hk, turn.
Rows 2–3: Ch 3, dc in each st
across, turn.
Row 4: Ch 2, 3-dc dec over next
3 dc, ch 3, sl st in last st; working
across ends of Rows 1–3, (ch 3,
sl st in base of last st on next row)
3 times; do not fasten off.

First stem
Ch 5, sl st in top of one cherry,
sl st in each ch of ch-5, sl st bet
leaves.

Second stem
Ch 7, sl st in top of one cherry,
sl st in each ch of ch-7, sl st bet
leaves.

Third stem
Ch 9, sl st in top of one cherry,
sl st in each ch of ch-9, sl st bet
leaves.

Fourth stem
Make same as second stem.

Fifth stem
Make same as first stem.
Fasten off.

FINISHING
Sew stems to purse as shown in
photograph below.

SCRAP-YARN TOTE

NEEDED ITEMS
- Yarn:

    A—several yards each of five or more yarns in varying
    weights, textures, and shades. Mix colors or select
    shades in the same color family.

    B—eyelash or novelty (50 yds)
- Crochet hook: I

Designed by Whitney Christmas

GAUGE
Approximately 4–6 sc per inch, depending on yarn used

SIZE
7" wide x 7" high plus handle

SPECIAL NOTES:
- Work with 1 strand worsted and bulky weight yarns at a time, and hold two or more strands tog if working with sport weight, baby weight, sock weight, or threads.
- To chg yarns, work to end of rnd but do not pl hk thr final 2 lps on hk of last sc; drop yarn to back of work and pick up new yarn, pl new yarn thr 2 lps on hk, sl st in first sc. Cont next rnd with new yarn.
- If you intend to use a particular yarn again within 2–5 rows, do not cut when chging yarns. Hold it to the inside of purse until you are ready to use it again, then pick it up, leaving enough slack not to pl when bag is stretched.
- Work as many rows as desired with each yarn, creating stripes as desired.

INSTRUCTIONS

PURSE

Row 1: Beg at purse bottom with first yarn, ch 17, sc in second ch from hk and in each ch across. (16)

Rows 2–5: Ch 1, sc in each st across, turn.

Row 6: Ch 1, sc in each st across, do not turn.

Rnd 7: To start purse sides, ch 1, working in ends of Rows 1–6 down side, sc in end of each row across, sc in each st across opposite side of starting ch, sc in end of each row down side, join with sl st in first sc, do not turn. (44)

Rnds 8–23: Ch 1, sc in same st, sc in each st around, join. At end of last row, fasten off.

Rnd 24: Join eyelash yarn with sc in any st, sc in each st around and join.

Rnds 25–29: Ch 1, sc in same st, sc in each st around, join. At end of last row, fasten off.

STRAP

Row 1: Leaving tail for sewing strap to purse, ch 7, sc in second ch from hk and in each ch across, turn. (6)

Rows 2–36: Ch 1, sc in each st across, turn. At end of last row, fasten off, leaving tail for sewing.

FINISHING

Fold strap in half lengthwise; working thr both layers, join with sl st 3" from end; sl st in each st across thr both layers to within 3" of rem end. Fasten off. Sew ends of strap to sides of purse.

SACHET PILLOW

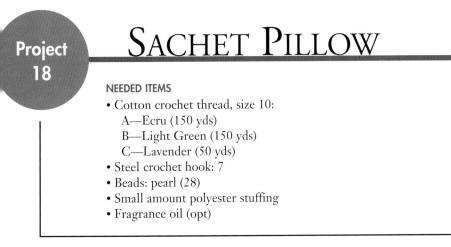

NEEDED ITEMS
- Cotton crochet thread, size 10:
    - A—Ecru (150 yds)
    - B—Light Green (150 yds)
    - C—Lavender (50 yds)
- Steel crochet hook: 7
- Beads: pearl (28)
- Small amount polyester stuffing
- Fragrance oil (opt)

Designed by Elizabeth Ann White

SIZE
6" sq plus 2" ruffle

SPECIAL STITCH
2-dc cluster: (Yo, pl up lp in next st, yo, pl thr 2 lps on hk) 2 times, yo, pl thr all lps on hk.

INSTRUCTIONS
INNER PILLOW HALF (MAKE 2)
Rnd 1: With B, ch 4, 11 dc in fourth ch from hk, join with sl st in top of ch-4. (12 dc)

Rnd 2: Ch 3, dc in first st, 2 dc in each st around, join. (24)
Rnd 3: Ch 3, dc in first st, dc in next st, (2 dc in next st, dc in next st) around, join. (36)
Rnd 4: Ch 3, dc in first st, dc in next 2 sts, (2 dc in next st, dc in next 2 sts) around, join. (48)
Rnd 5: Ch 3, dc in first st, dc in next 3 sts, (2 dc in next st, dc in next 3 sts) around, join. (60)
Rnd 6: Ch 3, dc in first st, dc in next 4 sts, (2 dc in next st, dc in next 4 sts) around, join. (72)
Rnd 7: Ch 3, dc in first st, dc in

next 5 sts, (2 dc in next st, dc in next 5 sts) around, join. (84)

Rnd 8: Ch 3, dc in first st, dc in next 6 sts, (2 dc in next st, dc in next 6 sts) around, join. (96)

Rnd 9: Ch 3, dc in first st, dc in next 7 sts, (2 dc in next st, dc in next 7 sts) around, join. (108)

Rnd 10: Ch 3, dc in first st, dc in next 8 sts, (2 dc in next st, dc in next 8 sts) around, join. (120)

Rnd 11: Ch 3, dc in first st, dc in next 9 sts, (2 dc in next st, dc in next 9 sts) around, join. Fasten off. (132)

ASSEMBLY

Holding halves wrong sides tog and working thr both thicknesses, join B with sc in first st, sc in each st around, stuffing lightly bef closing. Add a drop of fragrance oil to center of stuffing if desired.

ECRU LACE COVER HALF (MAKE 2)

Rnd 1: With A, ch 6, join with sl st in first ch to form ring, ch 3, 2 dc in ring, ch 2, (3 dc in ring, ch 2) 5 times, join.

Rnd 2: Ch 3, dc in first st, dc in next st, 2 dc in next st, ch 2, (2 dc in next st, dc in next st, 2 dc in next st, ch 2) around, join.

Rnd 3: Ch 3, dc in first st, dc in next 3 sts, 2 dc in next st, ch 2, (2 dc in next st, dc in next 3 sts, 2 dc in next st, ch 2) around, join.

Rnd 4: Ch 3, dc in first st, dc in next 5 sts, 2 dc in next st, ch 2, (2 dc in next st, dc in next 5 sts, 2 dc in next st, ch 2) around, join.

Rnd 5: Ch 3, dc in first st, dc in next 7 sts, 2 dc in next st, ch 2, (2 dc in next st, dc in next 7 sts, 2 dc in next st, ch 2) around, join.

Rnd 6: Ch 2, dc in next 7 sts, dc next 2 sts tog, ch 4, sc in next ch-sp, ch 4, (dc next 2 sts tog, dc in next 7 sts, dc next 2 sts tog, ch 4, sc in next ch-sp, ch 4) around, join with sl st in top of first dc (not in top of ch-2).

Rnd 7: Ch 2, dc in next 6 sts, dc next 2 sts tog, ch 4, (sc in next ch-sp, ch 4) 2 times, *dc next 2 sts tog, dc in next 5 sts, dc next 2 sts tog, ch 4, (sc in next ch-sp, ch 4) 2 times; rep from * around, join with sl st in top of first dc.

Rnd 8: Ch 2, dc in next 4 sts, dc

next 2 sts tog, ch 4, (sc in next ch-sp, ch 4) 3 times, *dc next 2 sts tog, dc in next 3 sts, dc next 2 sts tog, ch 4, (sc in next ch-sp, ch 4) 3 times; rep from * around, join with sl st in top of first dc.

Rnd 9: Ch 2, dc in next 2 sts, dc next 2 sts tog, ch 4, (sc in next ch-sp, ch 4) 4 times, *dc next 2 sts tog, dc in next st, dc next 2 sts tog, ch 4, (sc in next ch-sp, ch 4) 4 times; rep from * around, join with sl st in top of first dc.

Rnd 10: Ch 2, dc next 2 sts tog, ch 4, (sc in next ch-sp, ch 4) 5 times, *dc next 3 sts tog, ch 4, (sc in next ch-sp, ch 4) 5 times; rep from * around, join.

Rnd 11: Sl st to center of first ch-4 sp, (ch 1, sc) in same sp, ch 4, (sc in next ch sp, ch 4) around, join. Fasten off.

RUFFLE

Rnd 1: Holding both lace sides wrong sides tog, join A with sc in first sp, (ch 5, sc, ch 5) in same sp, (sc, ch 5, sc, ch 5) in each ch-sp around ending last rep with ch 2, dc in first sc.

Rnds 2–3: Ch 1, sc in first sp, (ch 5, sc in next ch-sp) around ending with ch 2, dc in first sc.

Rnd 4: Ch 1, sc in first ch sp, ch 1, (tr, ch 1) 7 times in next ch-sp, *sc in next ch-sp, (tr, ch 1) 7 times in next ch-sp; rep from * around, join. Fasten off.

Rnd 5: Join B with sc in first ch-sp, (ch 3, sc in next ch-sp) 7 times, *sc in next ch-sp, (ch 3, sc in next ch-sp) 7 times; rep from * around, join.

LARGE VIOLET

Rnd 1: With C, ch 6, sl st in first ch to form ring, ch 1, (sc in ring, ch 3) 6 times, join.

Rnd 2: Ch 1, (sc, ch 1, 3 dc, ch 1, sc) in each ch-sp around, join.

Rnd 3: Working behind petals, ch 3, (sl st in next sp bet petals, ch 3) around, join.

Rnd 4: Ch 1, (sc, ch 1, 5 dc, ch 1, sc) in each ch-sp around, join. Fasten off.

SMALL VIOLET (MAKE 18)

Rnd 1: With C, ch 3, 2-dc cluster in first ch, ch 2, sl st in first ch, (ch 2, 2-dc cluster in first ch, ch 2, sl st in first ch) 4 times. Fasten off.

FINISHING

Sew large violet to one side of sachet. Sew 10 beads to center of large violet. Sew small violets around edge of sachet with one bead in center of each violet.

ELEGANT EDGINGS

NEEDED ITEMS

- Cotton crochet thread, size 10 or size 3
- Steel crochet hooks: size 7 for size 10 thread or size 3 for size 3 thread
- ¼"–⅜"-wide ribbon (opt)
- Sewing needle
- Thread to match edging

SIZE

Edgings are approximately 1" wide when made with size 10 crochet cotton thread.

INSTRUCTIONS

EDGING #1

Row 1: Ch 11, dc in eighth ch from hk, ch 2, dc in last ch, turn.

Row 2: Ch 5, sk first ch-sp, dc in next dc, ch 2, dc in third ch of ch-5, turn.

Row 3: Ch 5, sk first ch-sp, dc in next dc, (ch 2, dc) 5 times in next ch-5 sp, ch 2, sl st in base of dc on row below, turn.

Row 4: (Ch 4, sl st in third ch from hk, ch 1, sc in next ch-2 sp) 5 times, ch 1, dc in next dc, ch 2, dc in next dc, ch 2, dc in third ch of ch-5, turn.

Row 5: Rep Row 2.

Rows 6–: Rep Rows 2–5 until edging is as long as desired, ending with Row 4. Fasten off.

EDGING #2

Row 1: Ch 11, dc in eighth ch from hk, ch 2, dc in last ch, turn.

Row 2: Ch 5, sk first ch-sp, dc in next dc, ch 2, dc in third ch of ch-5, turn.

Row 3: Ch 5, sk first ch-sp, dc in next dc, ch 2, 11 dc in next ch-5 sp, sl st in base of dc on row below, turn.

Row 4: Ch 1, sc in first dc, (ch 3, sl st in third ch from hk—picot made, sk next dc, sc in next dc) 4 times, picot, sk next dc, dc in next dc, ch 2, dc in next dc, ch 2, dc in third ch of ch-5, turn.
Row 5: Rep Row 2.
Rows 6–: Rep Rows 2–5 until edging is as long as desired, ending with Row 4. Fasten off.

FINISHING
Weave ribbon thr mesh along edge and tie in bow, if desired.

Using sewing needle and thread to match edging, sew edging to towel or desired item.

PRETTY BOOKMARK

NEEDED ITEMS
- Cotton crochet thread:
  - A—Blue (50 yds)
  - B—Yellow (50 yds)
- Steel crochet hook: 7
- Scissors

Designed by Elizabeth Ann White

SIZE
9" long

INSTRUCTIONS
FIRST FLOWER (BLUE)
Rnd 1: With B, ch 2, 6 sc in second ch from hk, join with sl st in first sc.

Rnd 2: Ch 1, sc in first st, ch 3, (sc in next st, ch 3) around, join. Fasten off.

Rnd 3: Join A with sc in first ch sp, (ch 1, 2 dc, tr, ch 3, sl st in top of tr—picot made, 2 dc, ch 1, sc) in same sp as joining, (sc, ch 1, 2 dc, tr, ch 3, sl st in top of tr—picot made, ch 1, sc) in each ch-sp around, join. Fasten off.

SECOND FLOWER (YELLOW)
Rnds 1–2: With A, work same as Rnds 1–2 of first flower.

Rnd 3: Join B with sc in first ch sp, (ch 1, 2 dc, tr, ch 1, sl st in picot of any petal on last flower made, ch 1, sl st in tr, 2 dc, ch 1, sc) in first ch-sp, (sc, ch 1, 2 dc, tr, ch 3, sl st in top of tr—picot made, 2 dc, ch 1, sc) in each ch-sp around, join. Fasten off.

THIRD–FIFTH FLOWERS
Working third flower with A, fourth flower with B, and fifth

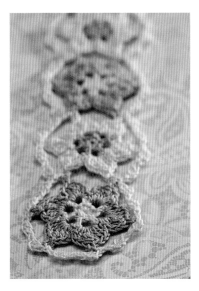

flower with A, work same as second flower.

EDGING

Join B with sc in first unworked picot on last flower made, *(Ch 3, dc in third ch from hk) 2 times, sc in next picot; rep from * around (joined picots count as one picot), join. Fasten off.

TASSEL

Wrap A 30 times around a CD case or 5" square of cardboard. Cut strands in half. Tie a 12" strand of B around center of all strands. Wrap another 12" strand of B around all A strands approximately 12" from top fold; tuck ends inside to secure. Tie tassel to one end of strip of flowers.

MAIRE'S ROSES AFGHAN

Project 21

NEEDED ITEMS
- Yarn:wool-blend worsted (11 skeins) (3oz/85 gr each)
- Crochet hook: J

GAUGE
Block = 6" sq

SIZE
Afghan = 43" x 55"

SPECIAL STITCH
Popcorn (pc): 5 dc in next st, remove hk from lp, insert hk in top of first of 5 dc just made, draw dropped lp thr, ch 1.

INSTRUCTIONS
BLOCK A (MAKE 31)
Rnd 1: Ch 5, join with sl st in first ch to form ring, ch 3, 2 dc in ring, ch 2, (3 dc, ch 2) 3 times in ring, join with sl st in top of ch 3.

Rnd 2: Ch 3, dc in next 2 dc, *(2 dc, ch 2, 2 dc) in corner ch-2 sp**; dc in next 3 dc; rep from * around, ending last rep at **, join.

Rnd 3: Ch 3, dc in next 4 dc, *(2 dc, ch 2, 2 dc) in corner ch-2 sp**; dc in next 7 dc; rep from * around ending last rep at **; dc in last 2 dc, join.

Rnd 4: Sl st in next dc, ch 4 (counts as dc and ch-1), sk next dc, (dc in next dc, ch 1, sk next dc) 2 times, *(2 dc, ch 2, 2 dc) in corner ch-2 sp**; ch 1, sk next dc, (dc in next dc, ch 1, sk next dc) 5 times; rep from * around, ending last rep at **; ch 1, sk next dc, (dc in next dc, ch 1, sk next

81

dc) 2 times, join with sl st in third ch of ch 4.

Rnd 5: Ch 3, dc in next ch-1 sp, dc in each dc and in each ch-1 sp around with (2 dc, ch 2, 2 dc) in each corner ch-2 sp; join. Fasten off.

BLOCK B (MAKE 8)

Rnds 1–3: Rep same rnds of Block A.

Rnd 4: Ch 3, dc in next 6 dc, *(2 dc, ch 2, 2 dc) in corner ch-2 sp**, dc in next 11 dc; rep from * around ending last rep at **; dc in last 4 dc, join.

Rnd 5: Ch 3, dc in next 8 dc, *(2 dc, ch 2, 2 dc) in corner ch-2 sp**, dc in next 15 dc; rep from * around ending last rep at **; dc in last 6 dc, join.

BLOCK C (ROSES) (MAKE 10)

Rnd 1: Ch 5, join, ch 4, (dc, ch 1) 7 times in ring, join with sl st in third ch of ch 4.

Rnd 2: Sl st in next ch-1 sp, ch 1, sc in same sp, ch 3, (sc in next ch-1 sp, ch 3) around, join with sl st in first sc.

Rnd 3: Sl st in next ch-3 sp, ch 1, (sc, 3 dc, sc) in same sp, ch 1, sk next sc, *(sc, 3 dc, sc) in next ch-3 sp, ch 1, sk next sc; rep from * around, join.

Rnd 4: Working at back, ch 1, sc in sc in rnd 2 bef joining just made, ch 4, (sc in next sc on Row 2, ch 4) around, join.

Rnd 5: Sl st in next ch-sp, ch 1, (sc, 5 dc, sc) in same ch-sp, ch 1, sk next sc, *(sc, 5 dc, sc) in next ch-sp, ch 1, sk sc; rep from * around, join.

Rnd 6: Working at back, ch 1, sc in sc in Rnd 4 bef joining just made, ch 6, (sc in next sc on Rnd 4, ch 6) around, join.

Rnd 7: Sl st in next ch-sp, ch 3, 6 dc in same ch-sp, *(dc, 3 tr, ch 2, 3 tr, dc) in next ch-sp**, 7 dc in next ch-sp; rep from * around ending last rep at **, join.

Rnd 8: Sl st in next st, ch 4, sk next st, (dc in next st, ch 1, sk next st) 4 times, *(2 dc, ch 2, 2 dc) in corner, (ch 1, sk next st, dc in next st) 7 times; rep from * 2 times, (2 dc, ch 2, 2 dc) in corner, (ch 1, sk next st, dc in next st) 2 times, join with sl st in third ch of ch-4. Fasten off.

BLOCK D (BUDS) (MAKE 14)

Rnd 1: Ch 5, join with sl st in first ch to form ring, ch 3, 2 dc in ring, ch 2, (3 dc, ch 2) 3 times in ring, join with sl st in top of ch 3.

Rnd 2: Ch 3, fpdc around next dc, dc in next st, *(2 dc, ch 2, 2 dc) in corner ch-2 sp**, dc in next dc, fpdc around next dc, dc in next dc; rep from * around, ending last rep at **, join.

Rnd 3: Sl st to corner ch-sp, ch 3, (dc, ch 2, 2 dc) in same sp, *dc in next st, sk next 2 sts, fpdc around fpdc, dc in second dc of 2

skipped dc, dc in top of next fpdc on Rnd 2, dc in next dc, fpdc around same fpdc on Rnd 2, sk next dc, dc in next st**, (2 dc, ch 2, 2 dc) in corner; rep from * around, working over sl sts on last rep and ending last rep at **, join. Fasten off.

Rnd 4: Ch 3, dc in next st, *(2 dc, ch 2, 2 dc) in corner, dc in next 5 sts, pc in next st**, dc in next 5 sts; rep from * around, ending last rep at **, dc in last 3 sts, join.

Rnd 5: Ch 3, dc in next 3 dc, *(2 dc, ch 2, 2 dc) in corner ch-2 sp**, dc in next 15 dc; rep from * around, ending last rep at **; dc in last 11 dc, join. Fasten off.

ASSEMBLY

Arrange blocks in a seven-by-nine block grid according to Maire's Roses Diagram on page 84. To crochet blocks tog, holding blocks right sides tog and working thr bk lps only on both layers, join with sc in corner and sc in each st along side. To sew blocks tog, hold blocks in same manner and whipstitch tog thr bk lps only.

MAIRE'S ROSES DIAGRAM

D	A	D	A	D	A	D
A	C	A	C	A	C	A
D	A	B	A	B	A	D
A	C	A	B	A	C	A
D	A	B	A	B	A	D
A	C	A	B	A	C	A
D	A	B	A	B	A	D
A	C	A	C	A	C	A
D	A	D	A	D	A	D

BORDER

Join with sl st in any corner, ch 3, (dc, ch 2, 2 dc) in same sp, *(ch 1, sk next st, dc in next st) 9 times, ch 1, dc in corner sp, ch 1, dc in corner sp on next block; rep from * around with (2 dc, ch 2, 2 dc) in each corner.

FRINGE

Wrap yarn around a 5" piece of cardboard to create fringe. Cut strands on one edge. Create each fringe with 3 strands in every ch-1 sp along edges of afghan.

To make fringe, with afghan right side up, insert hk from wrong side up thr ch-1 sp; fold fringe strands in half, forming lp. Insert hk in lp, pl thr ch-1 sp. Insert cut ends of fringe thr lp and pl to close knot. When fringe is in place, steam and trim evenly.

LACE BOOTIES & CAP

LACE BOOTIES & CAP

NEEDED ITEMS
- Crochet cotton thread: size 10 (250 yds)
- ³⁄₁₆"-wide satin picot-edged ribbon (46")
- Crochet hook: 6

Designed by Mickie Akins

GAUGE
Approximately 4–6 sc per inch, depending on yarn used

SIZE
Newborn

INSTRUCTIONS

BOOTIES (MAKE 2)

SOLE

Rnd 1: Ch 17, 2 hdc in third ch from hk, hdc in next 13 ch, 5 hdc in last ch; working in opposite side of starting ch, hdc in last 13 ch, join with sl st in third ch of beg ch. (34)

Rnd 2: Ch 2, hdc in same st, 2 hdc in next 2 sts, hdc in next 8 sts, dc in next 5 sts, 2 dc in each of next 6 sts, dc in next 5 sts, hdc in last 7 sts, join. (43)

Rnd 3: Ch 2, 2 hdc in next st, (hdc in next st, 2 hdc in next st) 2 times, hdc in next 8 sts, dc in next 6 sts, (2 dc in next st, dc in next st) 5 times, 2 dc in next st, dc in next 5 sts, hdc in last 7 sts, join. (52)

Rnd 4: Ch 2, hdc in next st, (2 hdc in next st, hdc in next 2 sts) 2 times, 2 hdc in next st, hdc in next 14 sts, (2 hdc in next st, hdc in next 2 sts) 5 times, 2 hdc in next st, hdc in last 13 sts, join. (61)

Rnd 5: Ch 1, sc in same st, (sc in next 4 sts, 2 sc in next st) 2 times, sc in next 20 sts, (2 sc in next st, sc in next 6 sts) 2 times, 2 sc in next st, sc in last 15 sts, join. Do not fasten off. (66)

UPPER

Note: To dc 2 sts tog, (yo, pl up lp in next st, yo, pl thr 2 lps on hk) 2 times, yo, pl thr all lps on hk. To dc 3 sts tog, work in same manner, except rep (to) 3 times. Use safety pin or yarn scrap for marker.

Rnd 1: Working in back lps only, ch 2, dc next 2 sts tog—beg shell made, (ch 2, dc next 3 sts tog—shell made) 21 times, ch 2, join with sl st in top of first st. (22 shells)

Rnd 2: Ch 3, 2 dc in same st, (sk next 2 ch, 3 dc in top of next shell) around, join.

Rnd 3: Ch 2, dc next 2 dc tog, (ch 2, dc next 3 dc tog) 10 times, place marker over last ch-2 made, (dc next 3 dc tog) 8 times, ch 2, dc next 3 dc tog, place marker over last ch-2 made, ch 2, (dc next 3 dc tog, ch 2) around, join. Fasten off. (9 shells between markers for toe)

INSTEP

Row 4: Join with sl st in top of first shell after first marker, ch 2, dc next 2 shells tog, (dc next 3 shells tog) 2 times, ch 2, sl st in next ch-sp on Rnd 3 (marked space), turn.

Row 5: Ch 1, dc in top of next 3 shells, ch 1, sl st in next ch-sp on rnd 3 (marked sp), ch 2, sl st in next ch-2 sp on Rnd 3, turn.

Row 6: Ch 1, dc in next 3 dc, ch 1, sl st in next ch-sp on Rnd 3 (ch-sp after marked sp). Do not turn. Do not fasten off.

TOP PORTION AND RUFFLE

Rnd 7: Sl st in top of the next shell, ch 5, (dc in next dc, ch 2) around, join in third ch of ch-5. (14 ch-2 sps)

Rnd 8: Ch 3, 2 dc in same st, 3 dc in each dc around, join.

Rnd 9: Ch 2, dc next 2 dc tog, (ch 3, dc next 3 dc tog) around, ch 3, join.

Rnd 10: Ch 3, 4 dc in same st, sc in second ch of ch-3, (5 dc in top of next shell, sc in second ch of ch-3) around, sl st in top of ch 3. Fasten off.

ROSE (MAKE 2)

Rnd 1: Ch 5, join to form ring, ch 1, (sc in ring, ch 3) 5 times, join with sl st in first sc.

Rnd 2: (Sc, 3 dc, sc—petal made) in each ch-3 loop around, join with sl st in first sc.

Rnd 3: Working behind petals and in ch-4 ring, ch 3, sc in ring under first petal, (ch 3, sc in ring under next petal) 4 times, ch 3, join with sl st in first sc.

Rnd 4: Ch 3, (sc, hdc, dc, 2 tr, dc, hdc, sc) in each ch-3 sp around, join with sl st in first sc.

Rnd 5: Ch 3, (sc in center dc of next petal on rnd 3, ch 3) 5 times, join in first sc. Fasten off, leaving tail for sewing.

FINISHING

Cut 12" ribbon for each bootie; weave thr Rnd 7 and tie in bow at top of instep. Sew rose to each bootie.

CAP

Rnd 1: Ch 6, join with sl st in first ch to form ring, ch 3, 26 dc in ring, join with sl st in top of ch 3. (27)

Rnd 2: Ch 2, dc next 2 sts tog, ch 5, (dc next 3 sts tog, ch 5) around, join. (9 shells)

Rnd 3: Ch 3, 2 dc in same st, sk next 2 ch, 3 dc in next ch, (3 dc in next dc, sk next 2 ch, 3 dc in next ch) around, join. (18 3–dc groups)

Rnds 4–5: Rep Rnds 2–3.

Rnd 6: Rep Rnd 2. (36 shells)

Rnd 7: Ch 1, sc in 1st st, sk next 2 ch, (5 dc in next ch, sk next 2 ch, sc in next st, sk next 2 ch) around, join with sl st in first sc.

Rnd 8: Ch 5, sk next 2 dc, sc in next dc, ch 2, (dc in next sc, ch 2, sk next 2 dc, sc in next dc, ch 2) around, join in third ch of ch-5. (72 ch-2 sps)

Rnd 9: Ch 3, 2 dc in same st, 3 dc in each sc and in each dc around, join. (72 3–dc groups)

Rnd 10: Ch 2, dc next 2 sts tog, ch 1, (dc next 3 sts tog, ch 1) around, join. (72 shells)

Rnd 11: Ch 3, 2 dc in same st, ch 2, [(sk next ch, st and ch), 3 dc in next st, ch 2] around, join. (36 3-dc groups)

Rnd 12: Ch 2, dc next 2 sts tog, (ch 3, dc next 3 sts tog) around, ch 3, join. (36 shells)

Rnd 13: Ch 3, 2 dc in same st, ch 2, (3 dc in top of next shell, ch 2) around, join.

Rnds 14–15: Rep Rnds 12–13.

Rnd 16: Rep Rnd 12. (36 shells)

Rnd 17: Ch 3, dc in same st, 2 dc in each ch and in each st across, join. Fasten off.

ROSES (MAKE 3)
Make same as roses on booties.

FINISHING
Weave rem ribbon thr Rnd 16; tie in bow on left side. Sew roses to center front.

TASSELED BERET & SCARF

NEEDED ITEMS

- Yarn: coordinating worsted
  - A—tweedy wool-blend (225 yds)
  - B—soft and fuzzy nylon blend (225 yds)
- Crochet hook: I
- Narrow metallic braid (1 yd)
- Glass bead with hole large enough to accommodate several strands of yarn

GAUGE

10 dc = 3
6 dc rows = 3 ‰

SIZE

One size fits all.

INSTRUCTIONS

BERET

Rnd 1: With A, ch 5, join with sl st in first ch to form ring, ch 3, 15 dc in ring; pick up B and drop A to back of work, join with sl st in top of ch 3. (16)

Rnd 2: With B, ch 3, dc in same st, 2 dc in each st around; chg colors at end of row as est, join. (32)

Rnd 3: With A, ch 3, dc in same st, dc in next st, (2 dc in next st, dc in next st) around, chg colors, join. (48)

Rnd 4: With B, ch 1, sc in same st, sk next st, 5 dc in next st, (sk next st, sc in next st, sk next st, 5 dc in next st) around, join with sl st in first sc. Fasten off.

Rnd 5: Join A with sc in center

dc of any 5-dc group, 5 dc in next sc, (sc in center dc of next 5-dc group, 5 dc in next sc) around, join. Fasten off.

Rnd 6: Join B with sl st in any sc, ch 3, *dc in next 2 dc, 5 dc in next dc, dc in next 2 dc**, dc in next sc; rep from * around, ending last rep at **; join. Fasten off.

Rnd 7: Join A with sc in first dc of any 5-dc group, sc in next st, 3 sc in next st, (sc in next 9 sts, 3 sc in next st) around, sc in last 7 sts, join.

Note: To dc next 3 sts tog, (yo, pl up lp in next st, yo, pl thr 2 lps on hk) 3 times, yo, pl thr all lps on hk.

Rnd 8: Join B with sl st in first sc of any 3-sc group, ch 3, dc in next 5 sts, dc next 3 sts tog, (dc in next 9 sts, dc next 3 sts tog) around, dc in last 3 sts, join, chg to A.

Rnd 9: With A, ch 3, dc in next 4 sts, dc next 3 sts tog, (dc in next 7 sts, dc next 3 sts tog) around, dc in last 2 sts, join. Fasten off.

Rnd 10: Join B with sl st in any st, ch 3, dc in each st around, join. Fasten off.

Rnd 11: Join A with sl st in any st, ch 2, dc in next st, (dc next 2 sts tog) around, join in top of first dc. (48) Fasten off.

Rnd 12: Join A with sl st in any st, ch 3, dc in each st around, join, do not fasten off.

Rnd 13: Ch 3, dc in each st around, join. Fasten off.

Rnd 14: Join B with sc in any st, *sk next 2 sts, 5 dc in next st, sk next 2 sts**, sc in next st; rep from * around, ending last rep at **, join. Fasten off.

TASSEL

Wind B nine times around a 5" piece of cardboard. Cut across one end; tie a separate strand

around center of strands. Wind metallic braid around tassel about ½" down from tie. Slip bead over tie. Using tie, sew tassel to top center of beret. Trim tassel to 4½".

SCARF

Row 1: Ch 23 with A, dc in third ch from hk and in each ch across, remove hk from lp, do not turn. (21)

Row 2: Join B with sl st in top of beg ch, ch 3, dc in each st across to last st; for last st, yo, pl up lp in last st, yo, pl thr 2 lps on hk, pick up dropped lp from Row 1, pl thr last 2 lps on hk, turn.

Row 3: With A, ch 3, dc in each st across, remove hk from lp, do not turn. (21)

Row 4: Insert hk in top of ch 3 at beg of previous row, pl up lp with B, ch 3, dc in each st across to last st; for last st, yo, pl up lp in last st, yo, pl thr 2 lps on hk, pick up dropped lp from previous row, pl thr last 2 lps on hk, turn.

Rows 5–61: Rep Rows 3–4, ending with Row 3.

Row 62: Join B with sc in first st, (sk next st, 5 dc in next st, sk next st, sc in next st) across. Fasten off, turn.

Row 63: Join A with sl st in first sc, ch 3, 2 dc in same st, (sc in center dc of next 5-dc group, 5 dc in next sc) across, ending with 3 dc in last sc. Fasten off, turn.

Row 64: Join B with sc in first st, (5 dc in next sc, sc in center dc of next 5-dc group) across, ending with sc in last sc. Fasten off, turn.

Rows 65–70: Rep Rows 63–64. Turn scarf; working on opposite side of starting ch, rep Rows 62–70.

ABOUT THE AUTHOR

Carolyn Christmas has spent most of her life involved with needlearts. A fourth-generation seamstress, quilter, and crocheter, she learned to knit and crochet at age 5. Growing up in sparsely populated West Texas, she often crocheted to pass the time on her 110-mile round-trip school bus ride. Far from the distractions of shopping malls, movie theaters, or even telephones and consistent television reception, Carolyn followed her mother's lead and filled her time with painting, sewing, and other creative pursuits.

Carolyn studied art, journalism, and political science in college, then started offering her original crochet, knitting, and cross-stitch designs to publishers in 1984 shortly after her second and third children, twin daughters, were born.

Since then, Carolyn has shared her love of crochet as an author, magazine and book editor, publisher, product designer, and teacher. From fashion to afghans, stuffed animals to doilies, she has created hundreds of crochet designs for publication.

Crochet is a family affair for Carolyn—she often collaborates with her mother, Dorris Brooks, as well as daughters Taryn and Whitney. Daughter Courtney often serves as hand model for Carolyn's how-to publications. Carolyn also collaborates with her husband, David Savage, in the creation of crochet hooks and other products for creative industry clients.

Visit Carolyn's Web site at www.carolynchristmas.com

METRIC CONVERSIONS

Inches	MM	CM	Inches	CM
⅛	3	0.3	9	22.9
¼	6	0.6	10	25.4
½	13	1.3	12	30.5
⅝	16	1.6	13	33.0
¾	19	1.9	14	35.6
⅞	22	2.2	15	38.1
1	25	2.5	16	40.6
1¼	32	3.2	17	43.2
1½	38	3.8	18	45.7
1¾	44	4.4	19	48.3
2	51	5.1	20	50.8
2½	64	6.4	21	53.3
3	76	7.6	22	55.9
3½	89	8.9	23	58.4
4	102	10.2	24	61.0
4½	114	11.4	25	63.5
5	127	12.7	26	66.0
6	152	15.2	27	68.6
7	178	17.8	28	71.1
8	203	20.3	29	73.7

Hook Conversion

US	Metric
B/1	2.25mm
C/2	2.75mm
D/3	3.25mm
E/4	3.50mm
F/5	3.75mm
G/6	4.00mm
H/8	5.00mm
I/9	5.50mm
J/10	6.00mm
K/10.5	6.50mm
L/11	8.00mm
M/13	9.00mm
N/15	10.00mm
P/16	11.5mm

INDEX